BRANCH LINE TO TENTERDEN

Vic Mitchell and Keith Smith

Cover picture: No. 3 *Bodiam* simmers beside the LNER poster boards suggesting holidays in Harrogate and York, in that last summer of peace before WWII. The guard in cloth cap reminds us of another casual aspect of the line - lack of uniform clothing. (S.W.Baker)

First published August 1985
Reprinted August 1988
Second reprint June 1997

ISBN 0 906520 21 5

© Middleton Press 1988

Design - Deborah Goodridge

Published by Middleton Press
        Easebourne Lane
        Midhurst
        West Sussex
        GU29 9AZ
        Tel: 01730 813169
        Fax: 01730 812601

Printed & bound by Biddles Ltd,
        Guildford and Kings Lynn

CONTENTS

GEOGRAPHICAL SETTING

From Robertsbridge the railway runs down the valley of the River Rother, crossing the latter beyond Northiam at which point the line leaves Sussex for Kent. Whilst the river turns south to enter the sea at Rye, the railway turns north to run close to a tributary, known as Newmill Channel, until reaching Rolvenden. The relatively level route in these broad valleys changes to a steeply climbing one (mainly 1 in 52) up to Tenterden, which is situated at about 200ft above sea level on an eastward extension of the Hastings Beds of sandstone. North of the town, these are penetrated by a short tunnel after which the line soon reaches the undulating plateau of the Wealden Clay, crossing the River Beult shortly before reaching Headcorn.

ACKNOWLEDGEMENTS

We would like to thank all those mentioned in the photograph captions for the assistance received. Our gratitude also goes to Mrs. E. Fisk, N. Stayon and our wives for help in production. We very much appreciate the cooperation of the editor of the *Tenterden Terrier*, P.D. Shaw; the Keeper of the Archives, E.J.R. Miller, and L. Darbyshire, who also produced the architectural drawings.

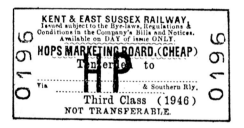

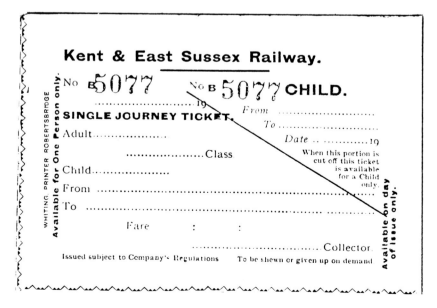

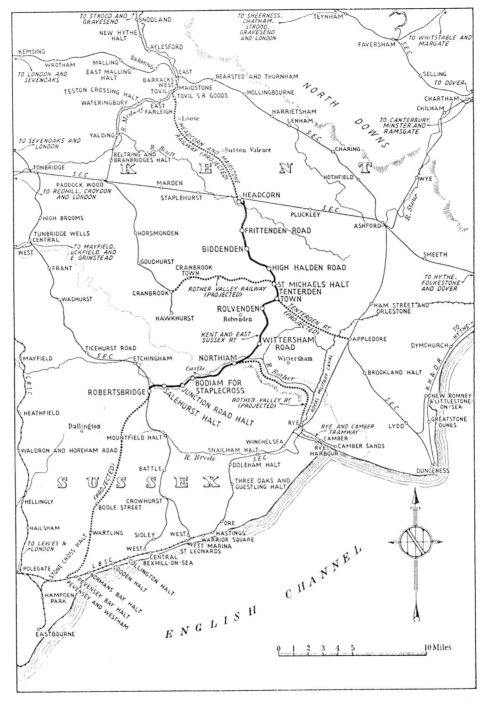

Map of the Kent and East Sussex Railway, showing also approximate route
of proposed extensions and associated railways

(Railway Magazine)

HISTORICAL BACKGROUND

The branch lines to Tenterden were located in an inverted triangle of main lines, the upper part of which was opened in 1842–3 and the other two sides completed in 1851–2. After prolonged local agitation, a successful Act was finally passed in 1896 for the construction of a branch from Robertsbridge to Tenterden. Later that year the Light Railways Act also received royal assent and consequently it was decided to build the new line under the provisions of this Act. This allowed for cheaper construction; economies being effected in rail weight (only 60lb/yd), signalling, level crossing arrangements and facilities for passengers at stations, although a speed limit penalty was suffered in consequence.

The terminus was over a mile from Tenterden, on the site of the present Rolvenden station. Goods traffic commenced on 26th March 1900 and passenger services on 2nd April. Operations were extended to a station close to the town on 16th March 1903. In the following year the company changed its name from the Rother Valley Railway to the Kent & East Sussex Railway in anticipation of a number of extensions. These are shown on the adjacent map but the only one to be completed was the branch from Headcorn which was opened on 15th May 1905.

During WWI, the railway came under Government control and when it was released, in 1921, compensation of £1487 was paid. In its early years the company had been moderately successful but in 1924 the northern section made a loss and by 1932 the whole line was unprofitable. The railway continued to operate in receivership and was controlled by the Railway Operating Executive during WWII.

Having been omitted from the Railways Grouping in 1923, it did not lose its independence until 1948 when it became part of British Railways. Closure was inevitable, the last passenger train being the 5.50pm from Robertsbridge on 2nd January 1954. It was composed of six coaches and required a banking engine to just beyond St. Michaels Halt. Goods services were retained from

Date	Merchandise		Coal & Fuels		Minerals		Livestock	
	Total	Orig	Total	Orig	Total	Orig	Total	Orig
1913	15126	5051	8946	—	7293	—	4819	4819
1914-18	x	x	x	x	x	x	x	x
1919	x	11151	x	86	x	208	x	2866
1920	x	10815	x	106	x	283	x	6759
1921	x	7661	x	30	x	227	x	4318
1922	15189	7996	11001	112	9515	1910	9628	7421
1923	17032	7005	10756	35	7704	1898	6540	5671
1924	17235	6344	12808	24	13639	2284	15746	13903
1925	15674	5580	12264	41	11705	1645	10270	8576
1926	12774	4289	7420	28	11933	2930	7880	6914
1927	13620	4981	12822	9	11797	1286	8605	7647
1928	14486	4896	11501	—	11116	487	10577	8363
1929	12213	3840	11285	—	19323	314	4986	4165
1930	10719	3471	12009	—	10164	217	8635	7165
1931	11202	3108	12161	—	8697	—	6443	5116
1932	10518	3406	12511	—	7684	214	7894	5043
1933	8350	2454	11075	—	6565	18	8007	6349
1934	8268	1977	12120	31	11416	44	8319	7088
1935	7398	1719	12240	—	6758	75	8880	8117
1936	6532	1835	13001	16	11872	173	6566	4954
1937	5401	1378	13577	45	10275	80	5767	4719
1938	4047	1002	14095	14	12573	71	5944	4640
1939-45	x	x	x	x	x	x	x	x
1946	x	4580	x	137	x	283	x	2116
1947	x	3897	x	62	x	167	x	1813

x Omitted by Authority of the Board of Trade

Tenterden southwards until 12th July 1961, during which time a number of trains were run for the benefit of hop pickers and four for railway enthusiasts.

After the complete closure, a preservation association was formed but it was faced with legal difficulties and new road schemes that would sever the remaining railway from the main line at Robertsbridge. Matters were finally resolved in 1971 when the Tenterden Railway Co. was incorporated with the aim of reopening the line between Tenterden and Bodiam, the company purchasing the land and track as far as Bodiam, for £60,000.

Public services at week-ends were resumed between Tenterden and Rolvenden on 3rd February 1974, the official reopening being performed on 1st June. Operations were extended in short sections in 1975, Wittersham Road being reached on 5th March 1977 and the station reopened on 16th June 1978. Trains ran to Hexden Bridge from 25th April 1983.

The railway is now almost entirely operated by volunteers and is being restored to commendable standards, with Bodiam the ultimate goal.

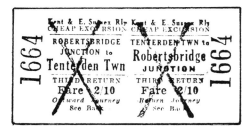

1. To promote its new railway, the company issued a set of six postcards in 1904, each showing an attractive view with the name of the nearest station in brackets.
(D. Cullum collection)

(5) TENTERDEN, OLD HOUSES IN HIGH STREET (TENTERDEN TOWN STATION).

2. Over 70 years later, the view remained equally attractive, if somewhat busier.
(L. Darbyshire)

Tonnage of Principal Classes of Merchandise 1920-34

	1920	1921	1922	1923	1924	1925	1926	1927	1928	1929	1930	1931	1932	1933	1934
Bricks	—	26	5	—	—	9	7	5	—	—	—	—	—	—	—
Iron and Steel	170	208	20	59	63	33	—	89	101	158	188	4	5	—	58
Limestone	—	—	—	6	—	—	4	—	—	—	—	—	—	—	—
Roadstone	—	—	—	2	—	—	—	—	—	—	—	—	—	—	—
Gravel and Sand	32	163	32	103	46	4	6	30	—	—	—	—	—	—	—
Manure	20	12	38	58	20	67	20	—	—	—	—	—	—	—	—
Grain	648	773	379	231	78	47	45	34	117	81	86	48	33	36	36
Hay	1943	1739	2524	1811	1945	1008	240	280	—	—	—	—	—	—	—
Potatoes	56	63	25	118	—	—	—	—	—	—	—	—	—	—	—
Seeds	—	—	—	12	6	7	7	—	—	—	—	—	—	—	—
Vegetables	—	—	—	—	25	48	15	20	—	6	5	—	21	—	—
Hops	—	—	597	493	800	630	548	386	—	—	—	—	—	—	—
Oilcake	—	—	—	—	—	—	—	—	5	—	15	—	—	—	—
Flour	178	77	76	20	62	24	15	26	—	—	—	—	—	—	—
Timber	1970	1074	450	301	344	605	565	1100	817	235	365	722	338	220	36
Wool	—	—	—	50	57	56	1	—	—	38	25	28	28	3	—
Empties	—	—	—	—	58	113	23	—	—	—	—	—	—	—	—

THE CHARACTER OF THE LINE

This was determined by the most notable individual character in the history of the line – H.F. Stephens. In the late 1890s he established himself in practice in Tonbridge as a civil engineer and in 1897, at the age of 29, became responsible for the supervision of the construction of the Rother Valley Railway. He was appointed General Manager in 1899 and Managing Director in 1900.

During this period, he was involved in the construction and management of a number of other minor railways, some of which were built under the 1896 Light Railways Act. All were subject to his unique form of economy – both in construction and operation. Whilst some were provided with new rolling stock initially, most of the lines existed with cast-offs from the main line companies or even second-hand industrial locomotives.

The RVR bought two new 2–4–0T Hawthorn Leslie locomotives and some new coaches. After the formation of the KESR, Stephens recommended that the company purchase another new engine to work the northern extension and the other proposed new lines. A massive 43-ton 0–8–0T was purchased and named *Hecate*. It was a white elephant from the outset, as it was too heavy to work south of Rolvenden and unnecessarily big for most of the trains. To compound the rare uneconomical act, Stephens ordered that the engine should be steamed occasionally to keep it in working order.

During World War I, Holman Fred Stephens acquired the rank of Lt. Col. in the Royal Engineers, and he subsequently became known on his various railways as simply "the Colonel". During the Amalgamation of the railways in 1923, he declined to allow his lines to become incorporated into one of the four new companies. It might have been better for the shareholders if he had accepted but we would have been deprived of one of the most unusual and fascinating chapters in railway history.

The Colonel disliked scrapping any equipment and so his lines became unique dumping grounds for historic relics. He resented paying water rates and so his lines became festooned with wind pumps. He could not tolerate the cost of using steam locomotives on light passenger trains and so his lines became inhabited by curious primitive petrol rail buses. All this was illustrated on the KESR and is seen in the following pages.

He was involved with 17 different railways and his empire continued to be ruled from offices between shops in Tonbridge, even after his death in 1931. He practised "locomotive swapping" and on a number of occasions engines were transferred between the KESR, the East Kent, the West Sussex, the Shropshire & Montgomeryshire and the Weston, Clevedon & Portishead.

The Colonel Stephens Museum is situated appropriately in Station Road at Tenterden, the town being equally appropriately the terminus of the only privately operated standard gauge passenger carrying Stephens line to survive. The displays include relics, tickets and photographs of many of the Colonel's lines together with his desk suitably covered with correspondence and equipment as if time had stopped still in 1931.

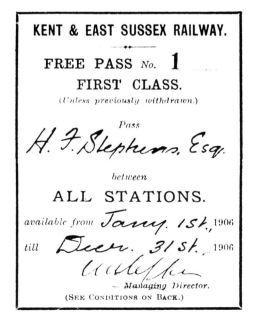

Pass no. 1 issued by Stephens to himself

PASSENGER SERVICES

Initially four weekday and two Sunday services were provided. By early 1905, the Sunday frequency had been doubled and an additional train ran on Wednesday evenings. With the extension of operations to Headcorn, the timetable is best described as erratic, there being a maximum of six return journeys over the full length of the line with a few short trips and some extra trains on certain days of the week. Regular Sunday services ceased during WWI. Frequency gradually diminished until only four trains appeared on weekdays on the northern part and three on the southern section in the final years. The timetable appears to have been designed to suit the railway staff, with many extra trips between Rolvenden and Tenterden.

Table 24 ROBERTSBRIDGE, TENTERDEN TOWN, and HEADCORN
Third class only

Miles from Robertsbridge	Down	Week Days only																		
		a.m	a.m		a.m		a.m	a.m	a.m		a.m		a.m		p.m	p.m		p.m	p.m	
								Saturdays excepted	Saturdays only		Saturdays excepted		Saturdays only					Saturdays only	Saturdays excepted	
	London—																			
22	Charing Cross ..... dep	..	..	..	..	..	..	..		..	1025	..	1034	..	..	..	..	3 25	4 20	..
22	Cannon Street ..... "	..	..	..	..	..	..	..		..	..	..	..	..	..	..	..	..	....	..
22	London Bridge .... "	..	..	..	5 45	..	..	..		..	1033	..	1043	..	..	..	..	..	4 28	..
22	Hastings .... "	..	..	..	7 40	..	..	..		..	1038	..	1038	..	..	..	..	5 10	5 10	..
—	Robertsbridge .... dep	..	..	..	8 15	..	..			..	1220	..	1230	..	..	..	..	5 50	5 50	..
1¼	Salehurst Halt	..	..	..	M	..	..			..	M	..	M	..	..	..	..	M	M	..
2½	Junction Road Halt	..	..	..	M	..	..			..	M	..	M	..	..	..	..	M	M	..
3½	Bodiam, for Staplecross.....	..	..	..	8 24	..	..			..	1232	..	1242	..	..	..	..	6 0	6 0	..
7	Northiam U	..	..	..	8 33	..	..			..	1243	..	1253	..	..	..	..	6 10	6 10	..
9½	Wittersham Road..........	..	..	..	8 42	..	..			..		..		..	..	..	..	6 17	6 17	..
12	Rolvenden.................	6 40	7 53	..	8 49	..	9 53		..	..		..		..	3 15	..	..	6 24	6 24	..
13½	Tenterden Town...........	6 45	8 0	..	8 55	..	10 0	1132	11 32	..		..		..	3 35	6 0	..	6 30	6 30	..
14½	Tenterden St. Michaels.....	..	M	..	..	..	M	M	M	..		..		..	M	M	..			..
15½	High Halden Road	..	8 10	..	..	..	10 10	1142	11 42	..		..		..	3 48	6 13	..			..
18	Biddenden.................	..	8 18	..	..	..	10 18	1150	11 50	..		..		..	4 6	6 23	..			..
19½	Frittenden Road...........	..	M	..	..	..	M	M	M	..		..		..	M	M	..			..
21½	Headcorn .... arr	..	8 30	..	..	..	10 30	12 2	12 2	..		..		..	4 22	6 38	..			..
67½	20 London (London Bdg.) arr	..	10 9	..	..	..	..	1 22	1 20	..	..	..		..	6B47	8 28	..			..
68	20 " (Cannon St.). "	..	10 14	..	..	..	..	..	..	..	..	..		..	6B57	..	..			..
69½	20 " (Charing Crs.) "	..	..	..	..	..	..	1 35	1 31	..	..	..		..	6SX3	8 41	..			..

Miles from Headcorn	Up	Week Days only																
		a.m		a.m	a.m.		a.m		p.m		p.m		p.m		p.m		p.m	
									Saturdays only		Saturdays excepted				Saturdays only		Saturdays excepted	
	London—																	
20	Charing Cross..... dep	..	..	..	9 15	..	11 15	..		..		..	3 15	..	4 34	..	5 29	..
20	Cannon Street.... "	..	..	6 22	..	..	..	..		..		..	..	..	..	..	5 40	..
20	London Bridge ... "	..	..	6 30	..	..	..	..		..		..	..	..	4 43	..	5 43	..
—	Headcorn .... dep	..	..	8 50	10 55	..	12 30	..		..		..	4 46	..	6 55	..	7 15	..
2	Frittenden Road...........	..	..	M	M	..	M	..		..		..	M	..	M	..	M	..
3½	Biddenden.................	..	..	9 6	11 8	..	12 43	..		..		..	5 0	..	7 8	..	7 28	..
5½	High Halden Road	..	..	9 19	11 16	..	12 52	..		..		..	5 9	..	7 17	..	7 36	..
7	Tenterden St. Michaels	..	..	M	M	..	M	..		..		..	M	..	M	..	M	..
8	Tenterden Town	6 55	..	9 38	11 25	..	1 10	..	4 15	..	4 35	..	5 24	..	7 27	..	7 47	..
9½	Rolvenden.................	7 0	..	9 45	..	..	1 15	..	4 22	..	4 42	..	..	..	7 32	..	7 52	..
12	Wittersham Road...........	7 7	..	9 52	..	..	..	..	4 30	..	4 50	..	..	..		..		..
14½	Northiam U	7 17	..	10 2	..	..	..	..	4 43	..	5 3	..	..	..		..		..
18	Bodiam, for Staplecross	7 27	..	10 12	..	..	..	..	4 56	..	5 16	..	..	..		..		..
19	Junction Road Halt	M	..	10 21	..	..	..	..	M	..	M	..	..	..		..		..
20¼	Salehurst Halt............	M	..	M	..	..	..	..	M	..	M	..	..	..		..		..
21½	Robertsbridge.......... arr	7 40	..	10 31	..	..	..	..	5 10	..	5 30	..	..	..		..		..
36½	22 Hastings............ arr	8 25	..	11 25	..	..	..	..	5 51	..	6 10	..	..	..		..		..
71½	22 London (London Bdg.) "	..		..	..	..	..	..	..	..	7 19	..	..	..		..		..
72½	22 " (Cannon St.). "	9 43	..	..	..	..	..	..	..	..	..	..	..	..		..	..	..
73½	22 " (Charing Crs.) "	..	..	12 8	..	..	..	..	6 33	..	7 32	..	..	..		..	..	..

B Via Redhill (Tables 20 and 40). Arr. Cannon St., 6 55 p.m. on Sats.
M Stops by signal to set down or pick up passengers
SX Saturdays excepted
U Station for Beckley and Sandhurst

Summer 1953

ROBERTSBRIDGE

3. One of the first photographs of the down platform was taken on 29th July 1888 and shows the gate keepers lodge near the double arm signal. The white fence behind the staff was eventually removed to allow the siding behind it to serve a bay platform for the Tenterden trains. The apparent lack of an up platform is explained by the fact it was built to the north of the down platform. (Lens of Sutton)

4. The platform was extended northwards and faced with timber instead of brick. In the bay is no.1 *Tenterden* with the RVR 1st class coach no.5. (L. Darbyshire collection)

5. The bay always lacked a run round, trains having to reverse out of the station to reach the loop, which can be seen on the map. The elegant tapered lamps and fenestrated chimney stacks are worth noting.
(Col. Stephens Museum)

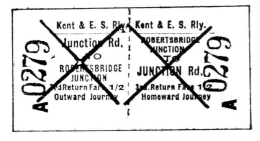

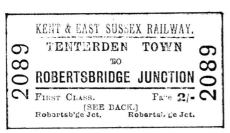

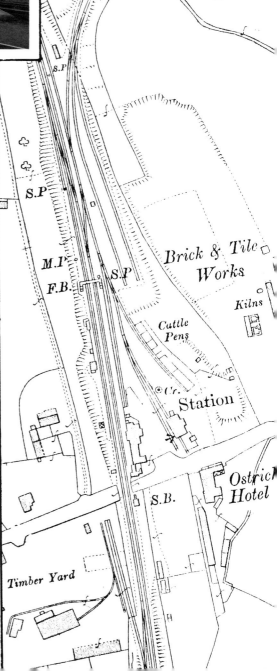

Long forgotten features of this 1909 map are the brickworks and the narrow gauge railway in the timber yard.

6. Whilst Driver Nelson Wood wanders off with his petrol can, the lone lady looks decidedly ill after her journey in the noisy, smelly and bumpy Shefflex railcar. The small wagon was attached when needed for parcels and luggage, as this pair of cars had no roof racks. (L. Darbyshire collection)

8. The coach nearest to no. 8 *Hesperus* was formerly Queen Victoria's saloon and was shown at the Great Exhibition in 1851. It was used as a 1st class coach on the KESR and had been hired on 27th June 1936 by the Oxford University Railway Society. It is seen here being propelled towards the loop in the company of an ex-LSWR 4-wheeled brake third. (R.W. Kidner/Oakwood Press)

SEASON TICKET.   First CLASS.

19**16** Kent and East Sussex Railway No. **340**

NOT TRANSFERABLE.   To be returned on Expiry.

Pass *L. Lefeaver Esq*

BETWEEN

Headcorn & *Tenterden*

From *Jan 1st 1916*, to *Dec 31st 1916*

Issued by *AG.*

W. Stephens

Managing Director.

7. A fine view of the congested SR goods yard in 1931, as seen from the footbridge. Look for the overtype steam wagon and the modernised platform lighting (gas). The coaches are ex-Great Eastern Railway 4-wheelers. (L. Darbyshire collection)

This season ticket was issued to a local government officer who used it to make journeys in the course of his work unlike most seasons which are used between home and work.

9. Both coaches and the Beyer Peacock "Saddleback" locomotive were built for the LSWR. The latter was acquired from the SR in 1932, in exchange for *Hecate*, the over-weight 0–8–0T described earlier. (L. Darbyshire collection)

10. "Why not plan your depot or works adjoining the railway where land is available at low rates," proclaimed the hoarding in 1938. The main lines are in the foreground and the connection to the KESR is in front of its small signal cabin. (S.W. Baker)

11. The round and square headed windows together with the four small archways give a prosperous appearance to the exterior of the station, which was designed by William Tress for the South Eastern Railway in 1851. (D. Cullum)

| 0228 | Kent & E. S. Rly.
TENTERDEN TN.
TO
ROBERTSBRIDGE
JUNCTION
FIRST RETURN
Fare **3/6**
[SEE BACK.]
Outward Journey | Kent & E. S. Rly.
Robertsb'dge Jct
TO
Tenterden Tn
FIRST RETURN
Fare **3/6**
SEE BACK
Return Journey. | 0228 |

| 2914 | ROTHER VALLEY RLY.
BODIAM
TO
ROBERTSBRIDGE.
10d. FIRST. **10d.** | 2914 |

| 2254 | KENT & EAST SUSSEX RAILWAY.
ROBERTSBRIDGE JUNCTION
TO
TENTERDEN TOWN
FIRST. Fare 2/-
(SEE BACK.)
Tenterden Town. Tenterden Town. | 2254 |

12. The scene on 14th September 1957 includes one of the then recently introduced 6-car diesel-electric sets bound for Charing Cross and Terrier no.32678 with a hop picker's special to Bodiam. It appears that the van was provided as there was no guard's compartment in either coach. (E. Wilmshurst)

14. By 1969, the former KESR 7-lever signal cabin had been given an imposing new name plate by BR. "Robertsbridge B" was by the level crossing and had 23 levers and a gate wheel. In the background is the BTH diesel-electric locomotive built in 1931 for shunting at Ford's new factory at Dagenham. It was then awaiting a permanent home on the KESR. (J. Scrace)

13. Two ex-SECR L class 4–4–0s are seen propelling a ramblers special over the branch connection on 18th October 1959. The five coach train had Terriers no.32670 and no.DS680 at opposite ends for the journey on the branch. (L. Darbyshire)

0091

2nd. Special Excursion 2nd.
"The Kent & East Sussex Special"
(C.M. 0091) 18th. OCT. 1959
Clapham Junction, London Bridge
or Victoria to
TENTERDEN TOWN
Via Kent & East Sussex Branch
AND BACK
(S)   (S)
For conditions see over

0091

HODSON'S MILL

15. The level crossing over the A21 was situated ½ mile from Robertsbridge station. In the foreground is a simple bridge over the River Rother and beyond the gates is the tower of a wind pump that had earlier lifted water from the river to a tank for locomotive supplies. (D. Cullum)

17. Hodsons were coal merchants as well as flour millers and so traffic inwards was quite heavy – 400 to 500 wagons per annum not being unusual. Here we see shunting in progress on 2nd January 1954. (D. Cullum)

⟵

16. Just beyond the water tower, partly seen in the previous photograph, was the only private industrial siding on the line, which was first used on 12th August 1903. The white gates protected yet another level crossing over the A21 which could be closed for lengthy periods during shunting operations. (A.J. Cowell)

046
S. E. & C. R. (SEE BACK
Available for 6 Months
Charing Cross to
ROBERTSBRIDGE
T] First Class 14/8
S. E. & C. R.
Available Day of issue
ONLY. (SEE BACK,
Robertsbridge to
CHARING CROSS
14/8 First Class [T
046

026
SOUTHERN RAILWAY.
Available for TWO
MONTHS. (SEE BACK)
Charing Cross to
ROBERTSBRIDGE
(T) First Class 21/2
SOUTHERN RAILWAY.
Available DAY of issue
ONLY. (SEE BACK)
Robertsbridge to
CHARING CROSS
21/2 First Class (T)
026

18. By 1959, grain was being imported via Avonmouth Docks and arrived in 20-ton bulk wagons. The sudden closure of the Tenterden branch to goods presented a problem to Mr Dadswell, the mill proprietor, so he bought P class no.31556 from BR; it arrived on 30th June 1961 and is visible on the left. When it was under repair, locomotives were hired from the Preservation Society – *Bodiam* and the BTH diesel for example. Traffic ceased in 1969, by which time the mill was owned by Ranks. (Lens of Sutton)

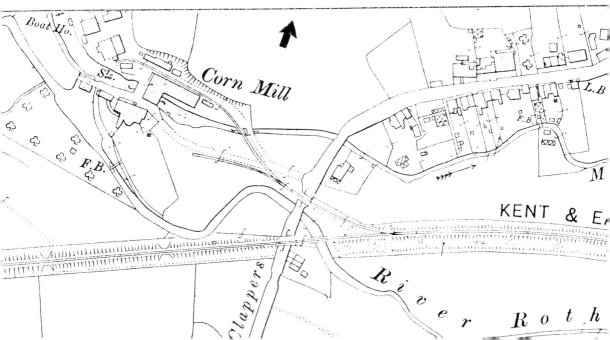

SALEHURST HALT

19. Initially, only a short siding was provided here for the benefit of the Bantony Estate. Eventually, this simple halt was provided for the use of the villagers. Here we see the 12.30 from Robertsbridge passing through on 2nd January 1954. (D. Cullum)

◄———

The 1909 map shows the two mill sidings, which remained unchanged during their existence. The longer one is seen passing over the mill tail race. Locomotives were not allowed to cross this bridge; it even collapsed under the weight of two vans in December 1928.

0343

KENT & EAST SUSSEX Rly

SALEHURST
TO
BODIAM

Fare 5d.   Third Class
(SEE BACK)

JUNCTION ROAD HALT

20. The 1909 map confirms that no siding was provided initially, it having been commissioned in February 1910. The word "Junction" was not a railway term but referred to the road which had been built to *join* two others – a short cut.
(D. Cullum collection)

22. Looking east on 2nd January 1954, we can see the halt in the distance and the then typical scenery of hop gardens. The current trend towards lager consumption has reduced the hop acreage dramatically. (D. Cullum)

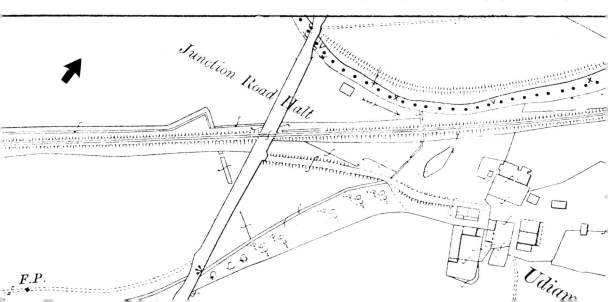

21. On 28th November 1953, passengers look out at the unusual operation of "tow roping", whereby the van from the middle of the mixed train was being hauled into the siding. (P. Hay)

23. A closer look at the halt on the same day shows it to have been reconstructed with concrete slabs, probably by BR. The oast houses, used for hop drying, were of the less common square type. (D. Cullum)

24. Junction Road is now the A229 and it was the level crossings here and on the A21 which were the main reasons for permanent closure west of Bodiam. The train is the LCGB special on 11th June 1961, which also had no. 32662 propelling. (S.C. Nash)

25. The Preservation Society was able to operate special trains occasionally between Robertsbridge and Tenterden, accompanied by BR staff. One such train is seen here on 11th April 1966, taking water from a stream by means of a portable petrol powered pump. (S.C. Nash)

ROBERTSBRIDGE, TENTERDEN TOWN, and HEADCORN.—Kent and East Sussex.

Miles from Robertsbridge.	Down.	Week Days.														Sundays.			
		mrn	mrn	mrn	mrn	mrn		aft	aft	aft	aft	aft		aft		mrn		aft	
	London—																		
	54 Charing Cross ......dep.	..	..	Saturdays only.	Mondays to Fridays.	9 30	..	2 25	..	Mondays to Fridays.	4 20	5 25		7 30	..	7 14	..	7 25	..
	54 Cannon Street ..... "	....	....			....	....	....	....		....	....		....	....	....	....	....	....
	54 London Bridge..... "	..	5 45			..	..	2 34	..		4 28	5 34		7 40	..	7 24	..	7 34	..
	56 Hastings .... "	....	7 40			10 40	....	2 53			5 10	5 10		9 10	....	9 10	....	8 40	....
	Robertsbridge ....dep.	..	8 15			11 15	..	3 50	Saturdays only		6 0	6 5	Wednesdays and Saturdays only.	9 45	..	9 45	..	9 15	..
1¼	Salehurst Halt....	....	M			M	....	M			M	M		M	....	M	....	M	....
2½	Junction Road Halt	..	M			M	..	M			M	M		M	..	M	..	M	..
3½	Bodiam, for Staplecross	....	8 25			11 30	....	4 0			6 19	7 0		9 55	....	9 53	....	9 25	....
7	Northiam W	..	8 35			11 55	..	4 10			6 20	7 10		10 5	..	10 5	..	9 35	..
9½	Wittersham Road	....	8 42			12 10	....	4 18			6 27	7 17		1012	....	10 12	....	9 42	....
12	Rolvenden	7 45	8 40	11 5	11 5	12 20	..	4 30		4 45	6 34	7 24		1019	..	10 20	..	9 50	..
13½	**Tenterden Town**	8 0	8 54	11 20	11 20	12 25	....	4 35	5 0	5 10	6 40	7 30		1025	....	10 25	....	9 55	....
14½	Tenterden St. Michaels	M	..	M	M	..	..	Saturdays only.	M	M	Mondays to Fridays.	Saturdays only.		..	..	Will run on August 28th, also September 4th, 11th, and 18th only.			
15¾	High Halden Road	8 10	....	11 30	11 30	....	....		5 15	5 25				....	....				
18	Biddenden	8 20	..	11 40	11 49	..	..		5 29	5 39				..	..				
19¾	Frittenden Road	M	....	M	M	....	....		M	M				....	....				
21½	**Headcorn 43**..........arr.	8 35	..	11 55	11 55	..	..		5 50	6 0				..	..				
67½	43 London (London Bdg)..arr.	10 6	....	1 13	1 17	....	....		7 20	8 13				....	....				
68	43 " (Cannon St.)... "	10 11	..	..	..	..	..		..	..				..	..				
69½	43 " (Charing Crs).. "	....	....	1 23	1 28	....	..		7 40	8 23				....	....				

Miles from Headcorn.	Up.	Week Days.													Sundays.			
		mrn		mrn	mrn	mrn	aft	aft	aft	aft	aft		aft					
	London—																	
	34 Charing Cross ......dep.	..	..	..	11 15	11 15	Saturdays only.	Mondays to Fridays.	Saturdays only.	4 30	..		..	..	Will run on August 28th, also September 4th, 11th, and 18th only.			
	34 Cannon Street ..... "	....	....	6 24	....	....				....	4 38		....	....				
	34 London Bridge ..... "	..	..	6 30	..	..				4 40	4 42		..	..				
	Headcorn ....dep.	....	....	8 50	12 32	12 40				6 35	6 35	Wednesdays and Saturdays only.	....	....				
2	Frittenden Road	..	..	M	M	M				M	M		..	..				
3½	Biddenden	....	....	9 10	12 45	12 53				6 47	6 47		....	....				
5¾	High Halden Road	..	..	9 20	12 54	1 2				6 56	6 56		..	..				
7	Tenterden St. Michaels	....	....	M	M	M				M	M		....	....	mrn		aft	
8	**Tenterden Town**	6 55	..	9 40	1 10	1 15	2 40	4 25	4 25	7 12	7 12		8 30	..	8 25	..	8 5	..
9½	Rolvenden	7 0	....	9 45	1 15	1 20	2 45	4 30	4 30	7 18	7 18		8 35	....	8 31	....	8 11	....
12	Wittersham Road	7 7	..	9 52	Mondays to Fridays.	Saturdays only.	2 54	4 40	4 40	Saturdays only	Mondays to Fridays.		8 44	..	8 39	..	8 19	..
14½	Northiam W	7 17	....	10 4			3 4	4 50	4 50				8 54	....	8 50	....	8 30	....
18	Bodiam, for Staplecross	7 27	..	10 16			3 14	5 0	5 0				9 4	..	9 0	..	8 40	..
19	Junction Road Halt	M	....	M			M	M	M				M	....	M	....	M	....
20¼	Salehurst Halt	M	..	M			M	M	M				M	..	M	..	M	..
21½	**Robertsbridge 54, 56**...arr.	7 40	....	10 32			3 25	5 16	5 16				9 15	....	9 15	....	9 0	....
36¾	54 Hastings ....arr.	8 25	..	11 25			4 18	6 38	7 19				9 55	..	10 1	..	9 33	..
71¾	56 London (London Bdg).. "	....	....	....			....	....	....				11 50	....	....	....	10 50	....
72¼	56 " (Cannon St.)... "	9 42	..	..			..	..	..				..	..	..	..	..	..
73½	56 " (Charing Crs) . "	9 53	....	12 3			5 16	6 43	7 0				11 59	....	11 27	....	11 0	....

M Stops by signal to set down or pick up passengers. **W** Station for Beckley and Sandhurst.

1938

BODIAM

26. Station Road was almost a mandatory subject for Edwardian postcard publishers. How well this one shows the remote rural location of the station, the village and castle of 1383 being ½ mile to the north. (Lens of Sutton)

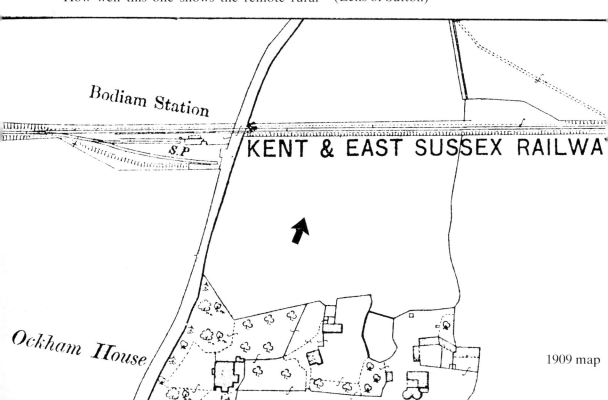

Bodiam Station

KENT & EAST SUSSEX RAILWA

S.P

Ockham House

1909 map

27. The siding in the foreground was added in 1910 and was approved for use by freight trains to pass passenger trains. It was never formed into a loop and seems never to have had a platform, although in this photograph it was of some use for the pump trolley. (Col. Stephens Museum)

28. Harry Batehup waits with the single line staff as a mixed train arrives on 14th March 1931, behind no.9 *Juno*, a Beyer Peacock 0–6–0 bought from the LSWR in 1914. The lamps were not lit with town gas but were supplied with acetylene generated in a nearby shed. (H.C. Casserley)

Kent & East Sussex Rly.

Visit BODIAM CASTLE and see
the MOAT and Ancient Buildings
Cheap Trips

	A.M.	A.M.	P.M
Leaving Hastings at	7 32	10 10	12 6
St. Leonards, Warrior Sq. at	7 35	10 13	12 9
Arriving at Bodiam	8 29	10 55	1 5

Fare Hastings, Adults ... 2/2 3rd class return
  ,,   Children under 12 years of age 1/1 ,,   ,,
  ,, St. Leonards, Warrior Sq., Adults 2/0 ,,   ,,
  ,,   Children under 12 years of age 1/0 ,,   ,,

CHILDREN UNDER 3 YEARS OF AGE WHEN ACCOMPANIED BY AN ADULT

MAY TRAVEL FREE.

AVAILABLE FOR RETURN BY ANY TRAIN SAME DAY.

TONBRIDGE
97290 APRIL 1927

H. F. STEPHENS,
MANAGING DIRECTOR·

29. On the same day, Ford railcar set no. 2 is seen roaring between Guinness' hop poles. These cars also emitted a loud ringing noise from their pressed steel wheels which acted like cymbals. (H.C. Casserley)

30. No. 3 *Bodiam*, later BR no. 32670 (seen in pictures nos. 24 and 25) shuffles past the bulky wooden signal post on 6th September 1946. Two coaches were unusual; broken signal glasses were not. (K. Nunn/LCGB)

31. Col. Stephens, a life long bachelor, made no provision for the comfort of ladies at his stations. Even the Gents had no WC. The rain water pipe on the end of the building was intended to flush the urinal. In times of drought, the smell was too much even for the flies. Such were the joys of light railway travel. (D. Cullum)

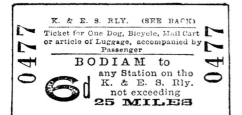

K. & E. S. RLY. (SEE BACK)
Ticket for One Dog, Bicycle, Mail Cart
or article of Luggage, accompanied by
Passenger
BODIAM to
6d any Station on the
K. & E. S. Rly.
not exceeding
25 MILES

0477

33. On 12th April 1958, The Branch Line Society hired four corridor coaches and two locomotives. Double heading was banned due to the weak bridges and so no. 32678 was at the back. Alas rain coats have shrunk since then. (L. Darbyshire) →

32. Looking west from the signal post in 1954, it is evident that the north siding did eventually gain road access and become more useful. The building on the right housed machines used in the hop gardens. (D. Cullum)

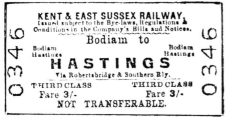

KENT & EAST SUSSEX RAILWAY,
Issued subject to the Bye-laws, Regulations &
Conditions in the Company's Bills and Notices.
Bodiam to
Bodiam   Bodiam
Hastings   Hastings
HASTINGS
Via Robertsbridge & Southern Rly.
THIRD CLASS   THIRD CLASS
Fare 3/-   Fare 3/-
NOT TRANSFERABLE.

0346

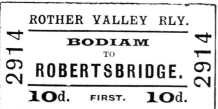

ROTHER VALLEY RLY.
BODIAM
TO
ROBERTSBRIDGE.
10d. FIRST. **10d.**

2914

Z 0614
KENT & EAST SUSSEX
RAILWAY
—
ROBERTSBRIDGE
TO
BODIAM
Fare **6d**
—
THIRD CLASS

0023
SOUTHERN RAILWAY.
WEEK-END.
Available to return on any
train on Sunday also on Monday
following the day of issue.
WE
to **BODIAM**
Via Robertsb'dge & K. & E.S.R.
1st. Class. Fare
**FOR CONDITIONS
SEE BACK**
SOUTHERN RAILWAY
WEEK-END.
Available on Day of issue only.
Bodiam to
Via K. & E.S.R. & Robertsb'dge
1st. Class. Fare
0023

34. Drewry diesel shunter no. 11223 (later D2250) is seen shunting on 15th July 1960. It had started working the branch in 1957, together with no. 11220. (R.N. Joanes) →

35. Preservation activity was evident at all stations in 1975. This 7½ ton Ruston shunter had been acquired from Plant Protection Ltd at Yalding three years earlier and the six-wheeled brake van had its ancestry on the SECR in 1898. (S.C. Nash)

Bradshaw 1910

ROBERTSBRIDGE JUNCTION and HEADCORN JUNCTION (1st and 3rd class).
Kent and East Sussex.
Eng., Gen. Man., and Loco. Supt., H. F. Stephens, Tonbridge.

	Down.	mrn	mrn		mrn	mrn	aft	aft	aft	aft	aft	aft	aft		aft		mrn	mrn	aft	aft
Miles	240 London (Charing Cross) dep.	....	....		....	9 10	1225		2 10	....	4 50	4 50		7 20		....	....	9 5	....	7 7
	240 " (Cannon Street) "	5 32	....		....	9 20	1238		2 20	....	5 05	0		7 30		....	....	9 12	....	7 17
	240 " (London Bridge) "	5 43	....		....	9 24	1239		2 25	....	....			7 35		....	....	9 17	....	7 24
	241 Hastings .... "	7 0	8 56		8 56	10 0	2 0		3 50	....	5 55	5 55		9 0		....	7 5	....	....	8 20
—	Robertsbridge Junction ..dep.	7 50	9 20		9 30	11 42	2 33		4 25	....	6 38	6 38		9 33		....	7 45	11 9	....	9 29
3	Junction Road, for Hawkhurst	....	Sig.		Sig.	....	Sig.		Sig.	....	....	....		....		....	....	Sig.	....	....
4	Bodiam, for Staplecross........	8 3	9 40		9 40	Sig.	2 43		4 38	....	....	....		9 43		....	7 55	1119	....	9 39
7	Northiam, for Beckley & Sand-	8 16	9 50		9 50	1142	2 53		4 52	....	6 55			9 53		....	5 1	1129	....	9 49
10	Wittersham Road ....[hurst	8 24	9 57		9 57	Sig.	Sig.		5 2	....	Sig.			Sig.		....	Sig.	1136	....	9 56
13	Rolvenden	8 35	1015		1025	1141	3 13		5 9	....	Sig.			10 8		....	Sig.	a	....	a
15	Tenterden Town........{ arr.	8 40							5 14	....	7 20			1017		....	8 25	1150	....	10 9
15	Tenterden Town........{ dep.	8 45			1142	3 14			5 35	....	8 10			....		....	8 30	....	6 40	....
18	High Halden Road............	8 52			Sig.	Sig.			5 42	....	8 18			....		....	8 38	....	6 48	....
20	Biddenden	8 59			1156	3 27			5 50	....	8 26			....		....	8 48	....	6 55	....
21	Frittenden Road..............	....			Sig.	Sig.			Sig.	....	Sig.			....		....	Sig.	....	Sig.	....
24	Headcorn June. 228,231 ..arr	9 10			1210	3 39			6 8	7 45	8 36			....		....	9 0	....	7 13	....

DIXTER HALT

36. This halt was opened on 25th May 1981 and the inaugural train is seen here composed of Peckett 0–4–0T *Marcia*, an ex-District Railway coach and a former LNWR 20-ton brake van. Services have since been operated spasmodically to and from Bodiam.
(B. Stephenson)

NORTHIAM

37. The RVR wagons indicate that this is a fairly early postcard view of the station, which was about a mile from the village it served. Unlike the intermediate stations on Col. Stephen's West Sussex Railway, illustrated in our *Branch Line to Selsey*, the corrugated iron buildings on the KESR mostly had platform canopies.
(D. Cullum collection)

39. This is the only view of an excursion train on the KESR that we have seen, but the photographer has unfortunately scratched the initials SECR from the panels of the leading coach although they are visible on the second one. (Lens of Sutton)

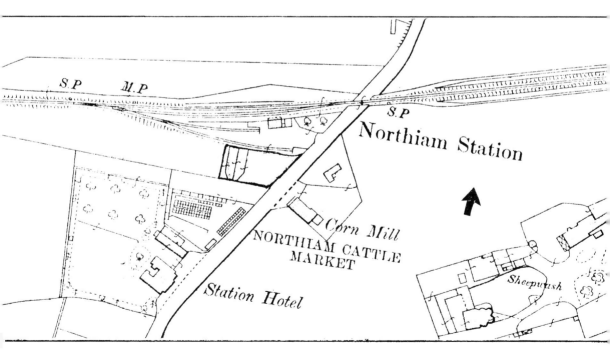

38. This postcard, dated 1907, shows the loop and second platform. It was the only station south of Tenterden with such features. The 1909 map shows the proximity of the cattle market to the station, – each would have benefitted the other. No.3 *Bodiam* leads a set of ex-GER coaches. (D. Cullum collection)

40. The rural railway was truly the general carrier – faggots on the down platform and a pair of cast iron baths having arrived on the up. A pump trolley is about to cross the level crossing. (Col. Stephens Museum)

Livestock Originating on the Line

Date	Horses	Cattle	Calves	Sheep	Pigs	Misc.
1913	—	955	239	3558	67	—
1914-18	x	x	x	x	x	x
1919	8	337	111	2294	116	—
1920	24	496	166	5391	682	—
1921	30	636	136	2952	564	—
1922	2	1035	180	5522	682	—
1923	—	1147	69	3998	457	—
1924	13	917	130	12063	780	—
1925	20	1138	106	6727	585	—
1926	6	834	52	5930	92	—
1927	—	933	27	6643	44	—
1928	6	866	93	1386	12	—
1929	—	497	32	3623	13	—
1930	2	1537	121	5460	16	—
1931	2	847	25	4242	—	—
1932	1	612	115	4311	4	—
1933	4	894	117	5292	41	1
1934	—	1145	107	5379	457	—
1935	—	1251	70	5623	1173	—
1936	—	732	83	2875	1264	—
1937	4	272	66	4281	96	—
1938	—	614	155	3871	—	—
1939-45	x	x	x	x	x	x
1946	—	281	7	1828	—	—
1947	—	186	31	1596	—	—

x Omitted by Authority of the Board of Trade

41. To this day, trespass signs often reveal something about the history of a railway. Looking east in 1938, less than a mile from the county boundary. (S.W. Baker)

42. Viewed from the level crossing, again in 1938, the down line seems little used, occupied by a single horse box. Eventually, the loop ceased to be used; the platform disappeared and so did the little rotating shunt signal in the foreground. (S.W. Baker)

KENT & EAST SUSSEX RAILWAY.

6050 ROBERTSBRIDGE JUNCTION 6050
TO
NORTHIAM

FIRST.   Fare 1/1
        (SEE BACK.)
Northiam.   Northiam.

KENT & EAST SUSSEX RAILWAY.

6162 NORTHIAM 6162
TO
HEADCORN JUNCTION

2/2 FIRST CLASS. 2/2
        [SEE BACK.]
Headcorn Jct.   Headcorn Jct.

TRAIN IS SINKING IN MARSH

AN engine, derailed on the Kent and East Sussex light railway at Wittersham, near Rye, is sinking into marshy ground.

If—as is thought—it proves impossible to get a heavy breakdown crane to the spot, the locomotive may have to be abandoned.

The engine and a coach were derailed by a subsidence. There were no passengers and the crew escaped injury.

The line was cleared last night but all efforts to re-rail the engine failed

44. Many women and children from London attended the hop pickers camps, often for several consecutive weeks. At week-ends the railways were obliged to run "Hop Pickers Friends" specials to convey husbands and others for a break in the country. Regrettably, excessive drinking of some, spoilt the pleasure of others. This is the 6.15pm special to London Bridge on 11th September 1949. (S.C. Nash)

43. In April 1949, Terrier no. 32678 left the track, owing to its settlement, east of the station. Despite the local reporter's pessimism, the engine was still at work on the line in 1958, when it was transferred to the Hayling branch. It survives today, having been on display at Butlins Minehead Holiday Camp for several years. (S.C. Nash)

KENT & EAST SUSSEX RAILWAY.

0421 | **HEADCORN JUNCTION** | 0421
TO
NORTHIAM
FIRST. Fare 2/7
(SEE BACK.)
Northiam. Northiam.

Kent & E. S. Rly.	Kent & E. S. Rly.
0305 Northiam TO **HEADCORN JUNCTION.** FIRST RETURN. Fare **4/4** [SEE BACK] Outward Journey.	Headcorn Junct. TO **NORTHIAM** FIRST RETURN. Fare **4/4** SEE BACK.] Return Journey. 0305

Kent & E. S. Rly.	Kent & E. S. Rly.
5185 **CHEAP.** Northiam TO **TENTERDEN T'N.** THIRD RETURN Fare **1/0** [SEE BACK Outward Journey.	**CHEAP** TENTERDEN T'N. TO **NORTHIAM** THIRD RETURN Fare **1/0** SEE BACK.] Return Journey 5185

45. The bridge over the River Rother is at the county boundary and is the longest bridge on the line, at 66 feet. It was extensively repaired in 1984 to allow an 18½ ton axle-load at 25mph. (Col. Stephens Museum)

WITTERSHAM ROAD

46. As Wittersham is over two miles from the station, a degree of frankness was apparent in this name and others further north. Unusual features are the square warning panels on the gates and the double armed signal, which was used to indicate to drivers if they were required to stop for passengers.
(L. Darbyshire collection)

47. As at Sidlesham on the Selsey line, the station building was curiously at right angles to the platform. Conversely, it was common practice in the days of ash platform surfaces for one part to be surfaced with timber to permit the easy movement of large milk churns by rolling them on their bottom edge.
(Col. Stephens Museum)

48. The 11.20pm from Robertsbridge on Easter Monday 1949 arrives, chasing its smoke. In front of the number is the staff holder which can be seen in use in picture. no. 44. (S.C. Nash)

49. Between February 1941 and August 1944, two rail mounted guns were stationed on the line, one here and one at Rolvenden. Each weighed 32 tons gross and fired 9.2ins. shells. Three GWR Dean Goods 0–6–0s, with condensing gear, were provided to move them when required. The gun here was only fired once and it broke all the windows in the station. (D. Cullum)

7564

KENT & EAST SUSSEX RAILWAY

WITTERSHAM ROAD

6d

PREPAID PARCEL

STAMP LABEL

| No. of Packages | Weight. |

TO

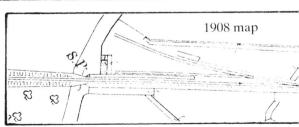

1908 map

50. Locomotives from other preserved railways have visited the line from time to time. *Fenchurch*, from the Bluebell Railway, is seen hauling its first passenger train on the evening of 15th September 1981. The ammunition store and gun crew shelter survive from WWII, in the former goods yard on the right. (B. Stephenson)

51. *Sutton* followed by *Bodiam* run round their train on 9th September 1984. The site had been levelled by BR and so the enterprising preservationists obtained materials from various sources. The station building came from Borth in Wales; the water tower from Shrewsbury Abbey station (terminus of the Colonel's Shropshire & Montgomeryshire Railway) and the copings from local platforms – Heathfield and Junction Road. (C. Hall)

K. & E. S. RLY.	K. & E. S. RLY.
3753	3753
Soldiers or Sailors in Uniform	Soldiers or Sailors in Uniform
CHEAP TICKET	CHEAP TICKET
Headcorn Jnct.	Wittersham Rd
TO	TO
Wittersham Rd	**HEADCORN JUNCTION**
Fare **1/1**	Fare **1/1**
Outward Half Not Transferable	Return Half Not Transferable

52. This photograph was taken during the first three years of the railway's life when this station was the terminus and was named "Tenterden". Points of interest are the RVR brake van for passenger trains; the coal heap on the ground (before a stage was built) and the curved roof on the locomotive shed. As at Selsey, this was later replaced with a pitched roof. The windmill, which was close to the water mill, can be seen above the coach roof. (Col. Stephens Museum)

53. Although a poor picture, it is worth including as it is the only one known to show 0–8–0T *Hecate* at work on the KESR. The cattle train is approaching Cranbrook Road, the wagons having been lime washed for reasons of hygiene. (Col. Stephens Museum)

The dotted line on this 1908 map indicates the stream leading to the Newmill Channel.

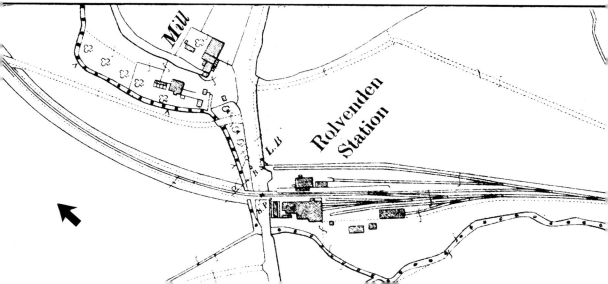

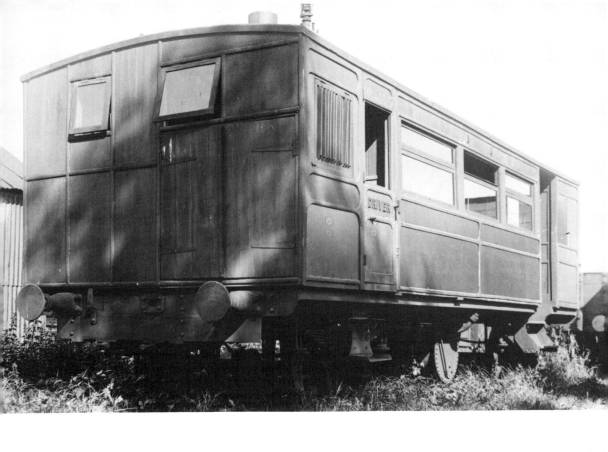

54. A dormant resident of the yard for nearly 30 years was this Pickering steam railcar, purchased in 1905 for £350. It was originally numbered as coach no. 16 but this was later changed to locomotive no. 6! It was a failure for several reasons – it was rough riding; it vibrated; it was hot and it constantly needed repairs. The garden shed doors on the front of the vehicle gave access to the boiler. The 150 gallon water tank can be seen under the body. The most useful component was the chassis, which can still be seen today, supporting the Rolvenden water tank.
(D. Cullum collection)

Engine thoroughly overhauled & repaired by S.E. & C.Rly.Coy at their marine works Dover 5/06

New Boiler purchased from messrs White Bros, Stratford and put in 7/07

New crank shaft made by Clarkes Crank & Forge Coy Lincoln and put in 8/08

New connecting rods made by J. Wright Tipton and put in Feb 1909

New set steel tubes put in boiler Aug 1909

New brass eccentric plummer block cap put on Aug 1909

Engine & Boiler overhauled March 1910

Engine & Boiler overhauled, tubes, new set May 1911

Engine and boiler overhauled and fractured staunchions repaired June 1913

Body left side overhauled and renewed June 1913

55. One of Stephen's more reliable machines – the ganger's "BUDA Velocopede Car". (Col. Stephens Museum)

56. There are many signs of neglect in this photograph taken in 1931, the year of the Colonel's death. From left to right is *Juno*, an ex-LSWR 0–6–0; *Tenterden*, with its clumsy wide chimney and the Ford railcar set no. 2. Tickets for this and other Stephens lines were printed in the shed next to the station. Another interesting detail is the unusual signal on the right. (L. Darbyshire collection)

57. No.3 *Bodiam* at the low point in its career in 1931 with embarrassing holes in its bunker in addition to a more obvious loss. Built in 1872, it has been in the Rother Valley since 1901, apart from 1954 to 1963 when it was used between Havant and Hayling Island. It is illustrated several times in this album and in our *Branch Line to Hayling*, running as no.32670. (H.C. Casserley)

58. A rare photograph, taken in 1932, of nos.1 and 2 in steam simultaneously, separated by Ford railcar set no.2. They were the first engines on the line and were scrapped in 1941. (Dr. I.C. Allen)

59. By 1933, no.3 was at the back of the shed undergoing a major rebuild which involved using many parts from the line's other Terrier, no.5 *Rolvenden*. (H.C. Casserley)

60. By 1938, the decaying boards above the doorways had been replaced and the rotting doors removed. On the left, the driver of un-named no.4 (ex-LSWR) looks down at his injector whilst no.8 *Hesperus* (ex-GWR) simmers in the sun. The unusual feature of the engine is the left-hand hung smokebox door. (H.C. Casserley)

61. The workshops were in a lean-to on the south side of the locomotive shed and were well equipped, for an independent line. The steam hammer and forge in the foreground are obvious – less so is the overhead shafting, from which flat belts took the power to drills and other equipment.
(Col. Stephens Museum)

62. No.3 again, with an ex-LSWR coach still with SR lettering. The hoarding by the letter box no doubt produced an income from the petrol company, who were otherwise helping indirectly to kill the railway. The Austin 10, parked by the concealed seat, adds to this 1937 scene. (H.C. Casserley)

63. A typical scene in the mid-thirties with (from left to right) the steam railcar; an abandoned cab (probably from no.9 *Rother*); an ex-LSWR coach; a Shefflex railcar; a train waiting in the station; three 4-wheeled coaches and, on the main line, a GWR four-door van and a SR horse box.
(Col. Stephens Museum)

The Printers Hut, drawn to the scale 4mm to 1ft.

64. *Rother* and *Juno's* dismembered remains stand unwanted, along with Terrier no.5, in the Autumn of 1938, after the hay rick in the background had been thatched. Line side grass was collected and sold to supplement the bankrupt railway's income. Mistle thrushes were noted visitors to this site (or maybe – sight), finding the spokes of *Juno* an ideal nesting place. (S.W. Baker)

65. A May 1939 view shows the shed on the left that was built in 1905 for the new steam railcar. The two sleeper walk-ways were erected to facilitate carriage servicing. To the right of the Shefflex railcars is the excessive fleet of cranes provided by the Colonel. The wide running boards on the railcars originally overhung the platforms so that after the car had filled with passengers, it was unable to move owing to the boards having jammed on the copings. (S.W. Baker) ⟶

66. A little later than, and a little to the left of, the previous view, we witness the end of the railcar era. They were a brave attempt to economise in operation, but their inability to haul any freight and their unpopularity with passengers led to their demise.
(Lens of Sutton)

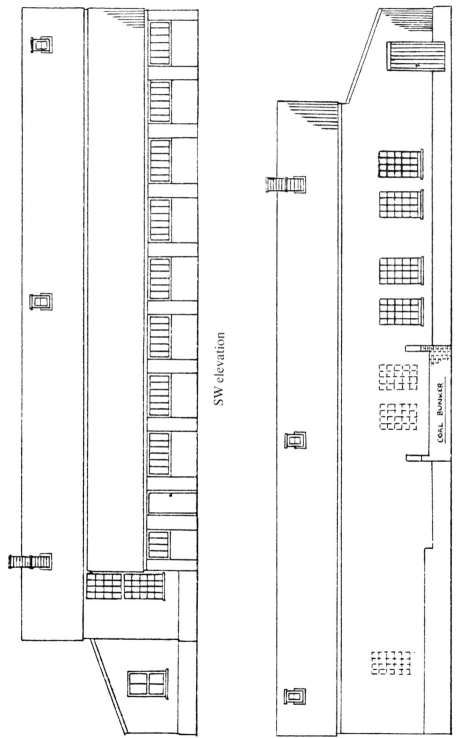

SW elevation

NE elevation

COAL BUNKER

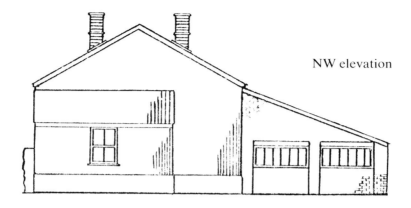

NW elevation

SE elevation

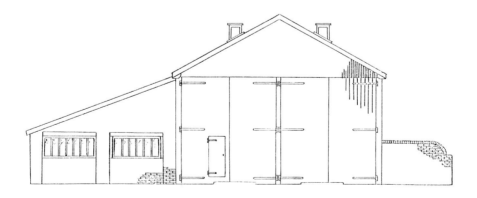

The locomotive shed, as drawn in 1955, to
the scale 2mm to 1ft.

67. Difficulty in finding a suitable replacement horse for the parcel delivery cart led to the purchase of a small lorry. This was the company's second vehicle – a 1936 Bedford. (Col. Stephens Museum)

69. A point of interest in this 1953 photograph is the narrowness of the road, the present gates being very much wider. A water column stands on the site of the previous tank, the replacement tank being the only item in this photograph, apart from a through line of track, to exist after closure by BR. (D. Cullum)

68. When KESR locomotives were unavailable, motive power was hired from the SR. This rare 1941 picture shows the black-out curtains on the cab and gives good views of the main line coaling and watering facilities, also the lean-to workshop. (Lens of Sutton)

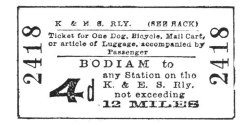

K & E. S. RLY. (SEE BACK)

Ticket for One Dog, Bicycle, Mail Cart, or article of Luggage, accompanied by Passenger

2418

BODIAM to

4d any Station on the K. & E. S. Rly. not exceeding 12 MILES

2418

70. BR listed Rolvenden as a sub-shed to Ashford and, after cessation of passenger services, the shed was closed and all motive power for the branch was supplied from St. Leonards. (D. Cullum collection)

The buildings at most other intermediate stations were of similar basic design. Scale – 4mm to 1ft.

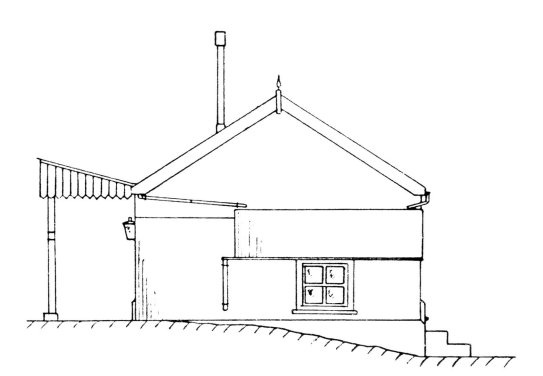

71. By 1955, the canopy had begun to sink. The raised platform was an unusual feature and was of benefit when loading or unloading milk churns and other heavy goods. It was also opposite the loading bay for road vehicles. (L. Darbyshire)

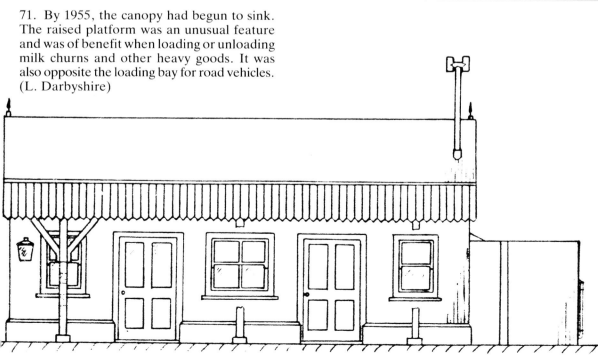

72. The land on which the shed and associated sidings stood was sold to a timber firm and so after the revival started, a new depot had to be built on the opposite side of the track. Here we can admire the achievements of volunteers. No. 10 *Sutton* is sporting flags on the occasion of the reopening of Newmill Bridge, on 5th March 1977. The saddle tank is a Hunslet 0–6–0 (numbered 26) and has since moved to the North Woolwich Station Museum. (J. Scrace)

73. Five ex-War Department Hunslets have operated on the line since it was re-opened in 1974. Here we see no. 23 climbing the 1 in 52 gradient from Rolvenden in the following year. Two years later, it was named *Holman F. Stephens* by Dr. Coiley, Curator of the National Railway Museum. (S.C. Nash)

74. A quarter of a mile south west of Rolvenden station, Col. Stephens personally financed the erection of about twenty timber framed and clad cottages for railway employees. This was an embryonic Crewe or Swindon which, like the branches of Maidstone, Cranbrook, Appledore, Rye and Pevensey, failed to grow. The area became known as Tin Town, owing to the Colonel's choice of roofing material. Charles Sharp, a fireman and railcar driver in the 1920s, is seen outside his cottage which was purchased from the Stephens estate for £75 in 1932. Photo date – 27th May 1985. (V. Mitchell)

75. About 1914, one of the "Ilfracombe Goods" engines, no. 7 *Rother*, sank between the rails just to the west of Tenterden station. The ex-GER coaches do not seem to have been badly damaged. (Col. Stephens Museum)

TENTERDEN TOWN

F.P.

Spring
S.B.

S.P.

S.P. *S.P.*

S.P.

Station

Sp.

F.P.

Windpump

Infant Sch.

G.Yd.
St. Mildred's Chʳ
(Vicarage)

The building in black on this 1908 map was the KESR stables and now houses the Col. Stephens and Town Museums.

G.Yd.

BISHOP'S LANE

School

SCHOOL LANE

School

STATION ROAD

Club

Brewery

Bk.

P.H.

Tks.

Bk.
P.Sta.
M.S.

P.H.

White Lion Hotel

P.O.

Fire Eng. Sta.

Zion Chap.
(Bapt.)

HIGH STREET

W.M.

Chap.

Tannery

Gas Works

76. Three postcard views give a good impression of the station in its early days. Posing for the camera is Terrier no.5 *Rolvenden* with one of the saloon coaches built for the line by Pickerings. Also posing is Mr. Arthur Taunt, the station agent – the KESR did not have station masters. (L. Darbyshire collection)

77. Turning the camera a little to the right gives us the opportunity to appreciate the unusually good relationship of the station to the town and also to see the termination of the fenced footpath from the opposite platform. (L. Darbyshire collection)

Station, Jenterden, from Church Jower.

78. The view from the church tower shows hoardings in the field beyond the station, five coaches and three cattle wagons. The paddock in the foreground later had cattle pens in it for storage of animals prior to their railway journey. (Col. Stephens Museum)

79. A postcard producer's howler that must have enraged the Colonel. The SECR did however have its own goods agent present at the station. He caused his employers to be fined on one occasion, when he despatched sheep in a coal wagon. To the left of *Rolvenden* is a Midland Railway wagon and, on the opposite platform, flower tubs reflect the mild prosperity of the period. (D. Cullum collection)

S. E. & C. RAILWAY STATION, TENTERDEN

80. In the centre of the picture is a rare view of the diminuative "signal box". The transposition of the wind powered water pump is evident in the next picture.
(D. Cullum collection)

KENT & EAST SUSSEX RAILWAY.
TENTERDEN TOWN
TO
ROBERTSBRIDGE JUNCTION
2090
FIRST CLASS.
Fare 2/-
[SEE BACK.]
Robertsb'ge Jct.
Robertsb'ge Jct.

KENT & EAST SUSSEX RAILWAY.
TENTERDEN TOWN
TO
HEADCORN JUNCTION
5008
FIRST CLASS.
Fare 1/6
[SEE BACK.]
Headcorn Jnct.
Headcorn Jnct.

Kent & East Sussex Rly.

British Legion (Robertsbridge Branch)

GRAND SPORTS MEETING

Whit Monday May 24th 1926
(EMPIRE DAY)

Special Cheap Return Tickets
TO

ROBERTSBRIDGE

Will be issued as follows by all Trains up to 2-0 p.m.

The Tickets are available for return on on day of issue only by any ordinary Train

Headcorn	......	2/9
Biddenden	......	2/6
High Halden Road	......	2/3
Tenterden Town	......	1/11
Rolvenden	......	1/8
Wittersham Road	......	1/3
Northiam	......	1/0
Bodiam	......	6d.

Children under 12 half fares   No luggage allowed

Tonbridge, April 1926

97186

H. F. STEPHENS,

Managing Director

81. A less common trainless view from the
east shows all three starting signals and a coal
delivery cart of the era.
(Col. Stephens Museum)

82. Between about 1916 and 1922, the
company offered passengers the use of their
bus to nearby destinations. Its discovery by
BR officials in 1948 at the back of the Station
Road stables led to its eventual preservation.
It is seen here in the museum at Clapham
from where it was moved to the National
Railway Museum at York.
(Col. Stephens Museum)

83. Although surviving for over a century, the former Royal saloon was less fortunate and was broken up. When photographed here in 1934, it must have been one of the oldest coaches in general use.
(Dr. I.C. Allen)

84. No.4, the un-named ex-LSWR "Saddle-back", clatters in with the 8.50am from Headcorn on 5th September 1946. Built in 1876, she appears to be showing her original wooden buffer beam. (K. Nunn/LCGB)

85. Two days later, the 11.15am from Robertsbridge passes over the level crossing hauled by P class no.1325, on hire from the SR. (K. Nunn/LCGB)

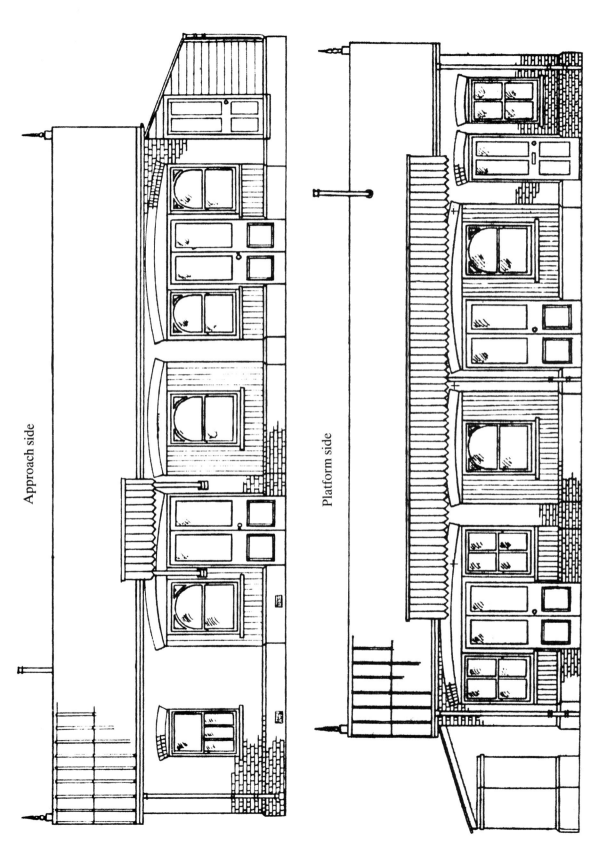

Approach side

Platform side

Detail of the awning supports, the positions of which are shown at + on the drawing opposite. The drawings are of the buildings in 1955 and are to the scale of 4mm to 1ft.

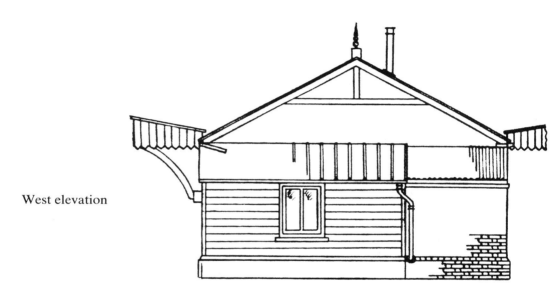

West elevation

East elevation

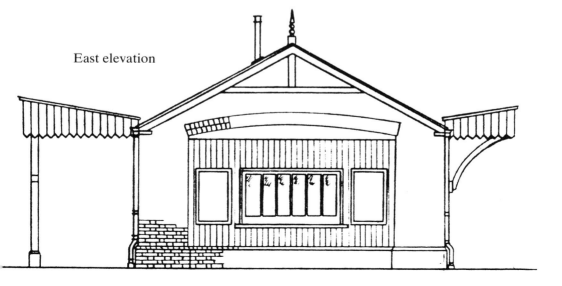

86. Built by the LBSCR as their no.55, this engine worked the last BR passenger train on the line and has since gained greater fame as the Bluebell Railway's *Stepney*. This 1951 photo shows parcels being loaded as the driver leaves the footplate, staff in hand. (Lens of Sutton)

88. The disused wind pump stands forlorn beside evidence of track renewals. A small stage can be seen, on the right of the picture, which facilitated loading and unloading of the adjacent emergency WWII stores. (D. Cullum)

87. The following three photographs show the conditions existing in November 1953. The boarded panel at the end of the building was, surprisingly, replaced by brick during the goods only period. (D. Cullum)

89. Facts to note in this picture are that the canopy covered only half the width of the platform and that the lights had been modernised – electric on concrete posts. (D. Cullum)

91. Tenterden was the only station on the line to have a goods crane. It was of 3-ton capacity and by 1955 mainly served to entertain local lads. (L. Darbyshire)

90. The black buildings on the left were erected to store wartime emergency supplies of flour and sugar. The railway carried other additional traffic during the war and was also used as an alternative route to Hastings. This photograph taken early on the last day of passenger services, shows extensive coal stock piles. (S.C. Nash)

←

In the late 1940's one could catch the 11.15 train from Charing Cross to Headcorn, change on to the K.&E.S.R. for Tenterden, where there was time for a pint and a sandwich before the afternoon train for Robertsbridge.

Consumption of the pint meant that one had to use a curious empty compartment at the end of an old L.S.W.R. coach containing nothing but a large hole in the floor, the management having removed the usual receptacle. The state of the track in those pre-B.R. days was deplorable, and the whole operation could be described as hit or miss. After arrival at Robertsbridge there was a wait of about half an hour before the arrival of a fast train from Hastings with a Pullman car, where one could sit in a coupé and be served with tea and toasted muffins under the pink silk-shaded lights, perhaps by Mr. Hubbard himself. A wonderful day's outing, alas, now totally unrepeatable.

London, W1   Tom Chalmers

Extract from a letter to the Editor of the
Tenterden Terrier

92. On 17th September 1978, nos. 10 and 24 begin the steep descent to Rolvenden whilst, in the background, the Steam and Country Fair benefits from a sunny day to raise additional funds for the railway restoration. (J. Scrace)

←

93. A notable visitor to the Steam and Country Fair in 1981 was the replica of *Rocket*, which steamed up the gradient from Cranbrook Road several times without difficulty. The signal box was formerly at Chilham, between Ashford and Canterbury West. (B. Stephenson)

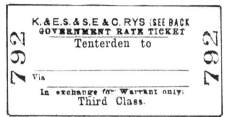

94. The construction gang take a break for photography, in 1903. The frame of a tipper wagon can be seen behind the horse that was drawing it. The temporary way appears to be 18" gauge, 2ft. being more popular for construction lines after WWI when much Government surplus material became available. (Col. Stephens Museum)

96. Several of the cottages are now occupied by railway volunteers. There is no trace of the halt today, the trackbed beyond the level crossing having become Orchard Road. (D. Cullum)

95. The gate for passengers was more obvious than the halt itself, when viewed from a southbound train in December 1953. (D. Cullum)

97. A little less than ¼ mile north of the halt was Shoreham Tunnel, which carried a minor country road over the railway. Class 01 no. 31065 is seen leaving the southern portal on the last day of passenger services. (S.C. Nash)

98. The north end of the tunnel was bombed on 18th August 1940, the bomb piercing eight feet of soil and the tunnel roof, finally exploding on the track. Normal train services were resumed the next day. (D. Cullum)

HIGH HALDEN ROAD

99. Looking south in the 1930s, we see evidence of the company's minimal telegraph system. The station was 1½ miles from High Halden church, being in the district known as Arcadia. (L. Darbyshire collection)

101. The hoarding in 1938 was announcing "electric refrigeration" at a time when the station did not even have electricity. The signal post was soon to serve another function – it carried the air raid siren during WWII. (S.W. Baker)

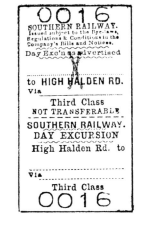

100. No.8 *Hesperus* was bought second-hand in 1914 and survived until 1941. The coach is ex-LSWR and the wagon owners are obvious. (L. Darbyshire collection)

102. Class O1s were almost exclusively used in the last years of the line, north of Rolvenden. The 41-ton locomotive, hauling a single coach, is seen creeping over the ungated "cross-your-fingers" level crossing. The building survives today as part of a nursery. (Lens of Sutton)

103. The stations on this half of the line were of similar design to the others but were clad with weatherboards instead of corrugated iron. The signals were used simply to indicate if the train was required to stop, the levers being visible at the base of the post. (L. Darbyshire)

BIDDENDEN

Biddenden Station

104. A postcard produced soon after the opening of the line shows no. 1 *Tenterden* running northwards with two brake vans from the North London Railway and two coaches bought from the Cheshire Lines Committee. The station was a mere ½ mile from the village. (D. Cullum collection)

The 1908 map does not show the fact that a gate was provided to field no. 643 direct from the platform. On Biddenden Fair Day, cattle could thus be loaded straight into the trains.

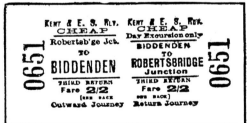

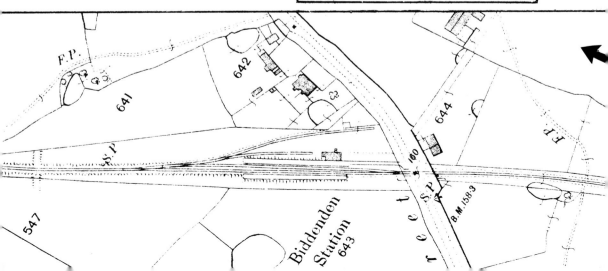

106. In bygone days, there were many passengers to the nearby sanatorium. Return tickets were valid for 12 months – treatment could be prolonged. By November 1953, there were often no passengers at all. (S.C. Nash)

105. This 1952 photograph shows that electric lighting had been provided, similar to that at Tenterden. The station agents house (extreme left) and the station both exist today, in private use. (D. Cullum)

107. In 1925, a train hit a brewery lorry on the level crossing and the brewers and the KESR were held jointly liable to pay £2147 to passengers for their injuries. Despite the Judge's comments, the crossing remained ungated 28 years later. Don't miss the tiny shunt signal. (D. Cullum)

108. No. 31064 was still at work on the branch on 3rd August 1955, this time sadly hauling a demolition train. (S.C. Nash)

FRITTENDEN ROAD

109. Being over two miles to the village, this remote station was another one to receive the suffix ROAD. The signal lamp and glasses divorced from the arms were reminiscent of the Southwold Railway, where the running signals were so arranged. (Lens of Sutton)

110. The neglected state of the permanent way and the platform edge are apparent in this 1938 photograph. The TELEPHONE sign indicated that the public were able to use the General Post Office line at the station. There was no coin box so the operator advised the station staff of the charge and the railway received a commission. (S.W. Baker)

111. By 1952, the track had received concrete sleepers and blocks, a system more commonly used in sidings. It also received visits from the weed-killing train but the approach path was overgrown due to lack of staff and usage. (D. Cullum)

112. Six weeks before closure, the driver looks out at a lone lady, with dog *and* pram, and probably wonders how she will manage on the replacement bus. The guard has apparently retired for a further period of rest. (S.C. Nash)

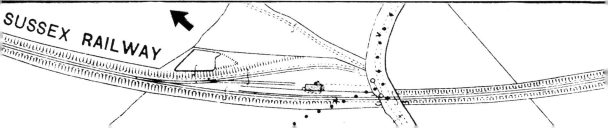

SUSSEX RAILWAY

HEADCORN

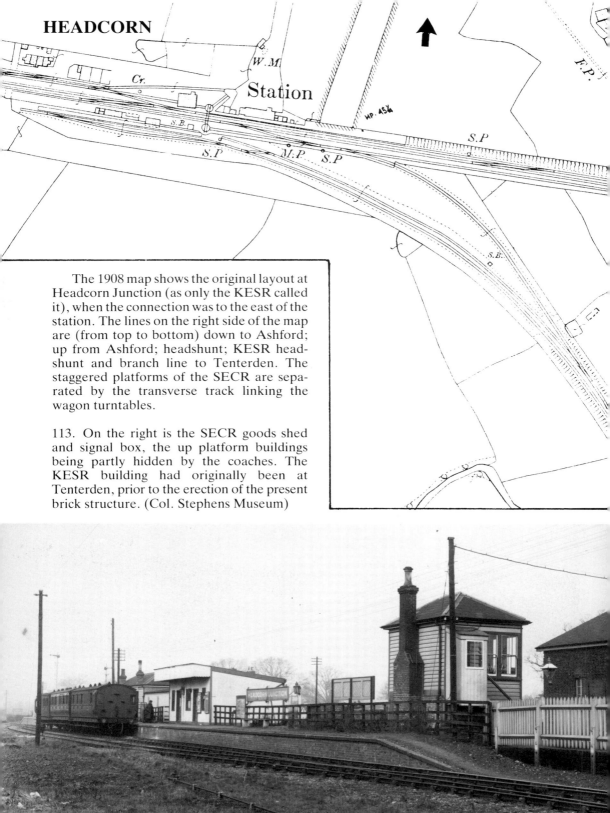

The 1908 map shows the original layout at Headcorn Junction (as only the KESR called it), when the connection was to the east of the station. The lines on the right side of the map are (from top to bottom) down to Ashford; up from Ashford; headshunt; KESR headshunt and branch line to Tenterden. The staggered platforms of the SECR are separated by the transverse track linking the wagon turntables.

113. On the right is the SECR goods shed and signal box, the up platform buildings being partly hidden by the coaches. The KESR building had originally been at Tenterden, prior to the erection of the present brick structure. (Col. Stephens Museum)

114. The SR decided in 1924 to quadruple their lines through the station. This involved demolition of their up platform; its reconstruction opposite the down platform; moving the KESR connection to the west of the station and the provision of a new platform for Tenterden trains seen here. The work was completed by 1930 and included a footbridge and new signal box for the main line together with a SR style signal for the branch. (L. Darbyshire collection)

115. No. 3 *Bodiam* stands behind the new SR up platform waiting shelter with ex-LSWR four-wheeler coach no. 1.
(Lens of Sutton)

116. An up express from Dover roars through on 10th September 1938, hauled by no. 782 *Sir Brian*, one of the King Arthur class. Two loops were provided for the KESR; one was used as a run-round, the other for stabling stock, as can be seen here. (S.W. Baker)

SOUTHERN RAILWAY

(12 46) 12v

Stock 787

TO

HEADCORN

KENT & E. S. RLY.
CHEAP
Robertsb'ge Jct.
TO
HEADCORN
Junction
THIRD RETURN
Fare 2/6
[SEE BACK]
Outward Journey

3270

KENT & E. S. RLY.
CHEAP
Day Excursion only
Headcorn Junct.
TO
ROBERTSBRIDGE
Junction
THIRD RETURN
Fare 2/6
SEE BACK]
Return Journey

3270

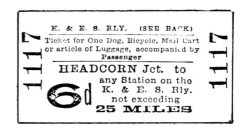

K. & E. S. RLY.   (SEE BACK)
Ticket for One Dog, Bicycle, Mail Cart
or article of Luggage, accompanied by
Passenger
HEADCORN Jct. to
any Station on the
K. & E. S. Rly.
not exceeding
25 MILES

6d

1117   1117

117. Mixed trains were run by the KESR without a brake van at the rear. BR introduced such vans to spread the brake load of loose coupled wagons. This P class tank is seen on hire on 16th July 1946. (S.W. Baker)

118. KESR no. 4 stands on the connecting line awaiting its final journey for scrapping whilst one of the SR's latest creations, no. 21C166 *Spitfire*, speeds towards Margate, on 25th April 1948. (S.C. Nash)

119. The original down platform buildings remain basically unaltered to this day. When photographed in August 1952, they were 110 years old. (D. Cullum)

Miles from Robertsbridge	Down	Week Days only																		
		a.m		a.m		a.m		a.m	a.m	a.m		a.m		p.m.	p.m			p.m	p.m	
	London—																			
22	Charing Cross.....dep.											9 25						3 25	4 20	
22	Cannon Street.... "																			
22	London Bridge.... "					5 45						9 35							4 28	
22	HASTINGS.......... "					7 40						1040						5 10	5 10	
—	**Robertsbridge**..........dep.					8 15			Saturdays excepted	Saturdays only		1120						5 50	5 50	
1¼	Salehurst Halt........					M						M						M	M	
2¼	Junction Road Halt........					M						M						M	M	
3½	Bodiam, for Staplecross....					8 24						1129						5 59	5 59	
7	Northiam W					8 35						1138						6 10	6 10	
9½	Wittersham Road........					8 42												6 17	6 17	
12	Rolvenden........	6 40		7 53		8 49		9 53						3 15				6 24	6 24	
13½	**Tenterden Town**........	6 45		8 0		8 55		10 0	1130	11 30				3Z35	6 0			6 30	6 30	
14½	Tenterden St. Michaels......			M				M	M	M				M	M					
15½	High Halden Road........			8 10				10 10	1140	11 40				3 48	6 13			Saturdays only	Saturdays excepted	
18	Biddenden........			8 18				10 18	1148	11 48				4 6	6 23					
19½	Frittenden Road........			M				M	M	M				M	M					
21½	**Headcorn**........arr.			8 30				10 30	12 0	12 0				4 22	6 38					
67½	20 **London** (London Bdg). arr.			10 9					1 22	1 14					8 28					
68	20 " (Cannon St.).. "			10 14																
69½	20 " (Charing Crs). "								1 35	1 24				6SX3	8 41					

Miles from Headcorn	Up	Week Days only																
		a.m	a.m		a.m.	a.m		p.m		p.m		p.m		p.m		p.m		
	London—																	
20	Charing Cross.....dep.				9 15	11 15						3 15		4 34				
20	Cannon Street.... "		6 22													5 40		
20	London Bridge.... "		6 30											4 43		5 45		
—	**Headcorn**..........dep.		8 59		10 53	12 30		Saturdays only		Saturdays excepted		4 46		6 55		7 15		
2	Frittenden Road........		M		M	M						M		M		M		
3½	Biddenden........		9 6		11 6	12 43						5 0		7 8		7 28		
5½	High Halden Road........		9 18		11 14	12 52						5 9		7 17		7 36		
7	Tenterden St. Michaels......		M		M	M						M		M		M		
8	**Tenterden Town**........	6 55	9 38		11 23	1 10		4 15		4 35		5 24		7 27		7 47		
9½	Rolvenden........	7 0	9 45			1 15		4 22		4 42				7 32		7 52		
12	Wittersham Road........	7 7	9 52					4 30		4 50				Saturdays only		Saturdays excepted		
14½	Northiam W	7 17	10 2					4 43		5 3								
18	Bodiam, for Staplecross.....	7 27	10 12					4 56		5 16								
19	Junction Road Halt........	M	10 21					M		M								
20½	Salehurst Halt........	M	M					M		M								
21½	**Robertsbridge**........arr.	7 40	10 31					5 10		5 30								
36½	22 HASTINGS........arr.	8 25	11 25					5 51		6 10								
71½	22 **London** (London Bdg). "									7 19								
72½	22 " (Cannon St.).. "	9 43																
73½	22 " (Charing Crs). "		12 5					6 38		7 32								

M Stops by signal to set down or pick up passengers. SX Saturdays excepted.

W Station for Beckley and Sandhurst. Z Arr. 3 20 p.m.

1949

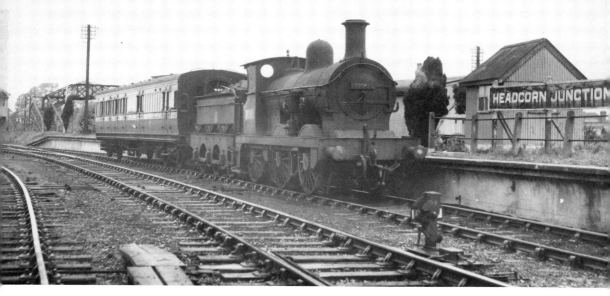

120. This peaceful scene at the northern end of the line will be remembered by many who visited this outpost of the Stephens' passenger railways in its final years. No. 31065 waits with the 10.55 on 7th November 1953 for the possibility of a traveller appearing. Your author, Vic Mitchell, has one such memory which is recounted below. (S.C. Nash)

I arrived at Headcorn from London on 9th September 1949 in time to catch the 12.30 pm departure. This was composed of O1 class no. 31048, an elderly brake third with four compartments, two wagons of coal and a goods brake van. There was one other passenger, an odd-shaped lady who waddled off at Biddenden, where some parcels were also off loaded. At Frittenden Road, I was amazed to see two signal arms on one post and no wires or signal box.

On approaching Tenterden, the train stopped in a cutting for no apparent reason. There was total silence and after a couple of minutes I saw the guard emerge from between the engine and the coach and climb onto the footplate. No. 31048 then left its train and solitary passenger, disappearing out of sight, quite silently.

Feeling as if I had been abandoned on a desert island, my thoughts turned to my stomach and so ate my lunchtime sandwiches and, without noticing, my teatime ones too. I then heard the ring of a coupling being removed. I must have looked out of the wrong side of the coach, as I saw no-one board it before it started to move. Eventually the guard's head appeared out the window as he brought the coach to a gentle stand in the platform. The locomotive was resting in a siding and the coal wagons and van soon arrived under gravity in an adjacent road.

A short gentleman, in sports clothes and Trilby hat, asked for my ticket. I explained that I was continuing my journey later and he shrugged his shoulders, as the next departure was at 4.35. However, as my train was due to terminate at Rolvenden at 1.15, I rejoined the coach when the locomotive reappeared, as I naturally wanted to visit the shed.

This accomplished, I decided to return to Tenterden on the 3.15 down train and re-commence my journey there. On arrival, a stern voice from under a Trilby hat said, "I thought you were continuing your journey, not returning here." I paid for a return to Rolvenden but sadly was not issued with a ticket.

A single coach appeared in due course (empty stock from Rolvenden) behind a Terrier. I regarded these as common little engines in those days and so I failed to note its number. On reaching my destination, Selsey, at 9.15 pm I felt that I had had an experience that would remain in the memory. It certainly has.

MP Middleton Press

Easebourne Lane, Midhurst. West Sussex. GU29 9AZ   Tel: 01730 813169   Fax: 01730 812601

. . . . . Write or telephone for our latest list . . . . .

BRANCH LINES
Branch Line to Allhallows
Branch Lines to Alton
Branch Lines around Ascot
Branch line to Ashburton
Branch Lines around Bodmin
Branch Line to Bude
Branch Lines around Canterbury
Branch Line to Cheddar
Branch Lines to East Grinstead
Branch Lines around Effingham Jn
Branch Line to Fairford
Branch Line to Hawkhurst
Branch Line to Hayling
Branch Line to Ilfracombe
Branch Lines to Longmoor
Branch Line to Lyme Regis
Branch Line to Lynton
Branch Lines around Midhurst
Branch Line to Minehead
Branch Lines to Newport
Branch Line to Padstow
Branch Lines around Portmadoc 1923-46
Branch Lines around Porthmadog 1954-94
Branch Lines to Seaton & Sidmouth
Branch Line to Selsey
Branch Lines around Sheerness
Branch Line to Southwold
Branch Line to Swanage
Branch Line to Tenterden
Branch Lines to Torrington
Branch Lines to Tunbridge Wells
Branch Line to Upwell
Branch Lines around Weymouth
Branch Lines around Wimborne

LONDON SUBURBAN RAILWAYS
Caterham and Tattenham Corner
Clapham Jn. to Beckenham Jn.
Crystal Palace and Catford Loop
East London Line
Holborn Viaduct to Lewisham
Lines aound Wimbledon
London Bridge to Addiscombe
Mitcham Junction Lines
North London Line
South London Line
West Croydon to Epsom
West London Line
Willesden Junction to Richmond
Wimbledon to Epsom

STEAMING THROUGH
Steaming through Cornwall
Steaming through East Sussex
Steaming through the Isle of Wight
Steaming through West Hants
Steaming through West Sussex

GREAT RAILWAY ERAS
Ashford from Steam to Eurostar
Festiniog in the Fifties
Festiniog in the Sixties

SOUTH COAST RAILWAYS
Ashford to Dover
Brighton to Eastbourne
Chichester to Portsmouth
Dover to Ramsgate
Ryde to Ventnor
Worthing to Chichester

SOUTHERN MAIN LINES
Bromley South to Rochester
Charing Cross to Orpington
Crawley to Littlehampton
Dartford to Sittingbourne
East Croydon to Three Bridges
Epsom to Horsham
Exeter to Barnstaple
Exeter to Tavistock
Faversham to Dover
Haywards Heath to Seaford
London Bridge to East Croydon
Orpington to Tonbridge
Sittingbourne to Ramsgate
Swanley to Ashford
Tavistock to Plymouth
Victoria to Bromley South
Waterloo to Windsor
Woking to Portsmouth
Woking to Southampton
Yeovil to Exeter

COUNTRY RAILWAY ROUTES
Bath to Evercreech Junction
Bournemouth to Evercreech Jn
Burnham to Evercreech Junction
Croydon to East Grinstead
East Kent Light Railway
Fareham to Salisbury
Frome to Bristol
Guildford to Redhill
Porthmadog to Blaenau
Reading to Basingstoke
Reading to Guildford
Redhill to Ashford
Salisbury to Westbury
Strood to Paddock Wood
Taunton to Barnstaple
Westbury to Bath
Woking to Alton

TROLLEYBUS CLASSICS
Croydon's Trolleybuses
Hastings Trolleybuses
Woolwich & Dartford Trolleybuses

TRAMWAY CLASSICS
Aldgate & Stepney Tramways
Bath Tramways
Barnet & Finchley Tramways
Bournemouth & Poole Tramways
Brighton's Tramways
Bristol's Tramways
Camberwell & W. Norwood Tramways
Croydon's Tramways
Dover's Tramways
East Ham & West Ham Tramways
Eltham & Woolwich Tramways
Embankment & Waterloo Tramways
Exeter & Taunton Tramways
Greenwich & Dartford Tramways
Hampstead & Highgate Tramways
Hastings Tramways
Holborn & Finsbury Tramways
Ilford & Barking Tramways
Kingston & Wimbledon Tramways
Lewisham & Catford Tramways
Maidstone & Chatham Tramways
North Kent Tramways
Portsmouth's Tramways
Reading Tramways
Seaton & Eastbourne Tramways
Southampton Tramways
Southend-on-sea Tramways
Stamford Hill Tramways
Thanet's Tramways
Victoria & Lambeth Tramways
Walthamstow & Leyton Tramways
Wandsworth & Battersea Tramways

OTHER RAILWAY BOOKS
Garraway Father & Son
Industrial Railways of the South East
London Chatham & Dover Railway

MILITARY BOOKS
Battle over Portsmouth
Battle Over Sussex 1940
Blitz Over Sussex 1941-42
Bognor at War
Bombers over Sussex 1943-45
Military Defence of West Sussex
Secret Sussex Resistance

WATERWAY ALBUMS
Hampshire Waterways
Kent and East Sussex Waterways
London's Lost Route to the Sea
London to Portsmouth Waterway
Surrey Waterways

COUNTRY BOOK
Brickmaking in Sussex

SOUTHERN RAILWAY
• VIDEO •
War on the Line